JAZZ IMPROVISATION SERIES

APPROACHING THE STANDARDS

by Dr. Willie L. Hill, Jr.

PREFACE

There are two groups of standards that help form the basic repertory used in jazz improvisation. The first group was created by jazz musicians directly from improvisation, experimentation and the analysis of musical forms, ideas and practices that were developed through study and the natural gifts of some of the greatest musicians of the twentieth century. This group codified jazz into chronological styles and provides concrete examples of its styles and concepts. The second group of standards is comprised of compositions written as popular songs during the first half of the twentieth century. Many of the composers of these songs were highly influenced by jazz composers and players. Jazz musicians also used compositions by composers who were not influenced by jazz because those compositions became excellent vehicles for jazz improvisation when the melodies were altered to fit jazz concepts.

In this series, Dr. Willie Hill has utilized compositions from both groups to give musicians a well-balanced selection of music to help the "fearful to the fearless" improve their jazz skills. He has provided a learning situation that is similar to a typical jazz gig setting and has included clearly written musical examples to demonstrate how an improvised solo might be constructed.

Every improviser is a composer who makes up melodies spontaneously. The model choruses give examples that can be studied, learned, broken into independent phrases and used to create other melodies that reflect more clearly what the improviser wants to say musically. Dr. Hill has given the player who uses this series an inside look at the jazz vocabulary, transcription opportunities, informative composer insights and a useful discography to help put the music into the context that is needed to improve his/her jazz skills. Whatever your instrument, you can have fun and learn a lot as you study the music, learn the melodies and play along with the excellent musicians on the enclosed CDs.

Dr. Billy Taylor

Editor: Pete BarenBregge
Production Coordinator: Edmond Randle
Technical Editor: Glyn Dryhurst
Finale Engraver: Mark Burgess
Art Design: Joe Klucar
Art Layout: María A. Chenique

TABLE OF CONTENTS

INTRODUCTION

Approaching the Standards, Volumes 1, 2 and 3, are part of the Jazz Improvisation Series. From the jazz novice to budding professionals, this play-along series is designed to help individuals build a melodic, harmonic and rhythmic jazz vocabulary. Eight classic jazz tunes are featured on each play-along CD for students to listen, analyze, transcribe and commit to memory. Each tune gives the player the opportunity to hear the jazz language performed by professional musicians as if they were performing at a real gig. CD icons are included to clarify the sequence of tracks in the book; observe the following:

A. First track for each tune
1. Head (demo)
2. Example improvisation (listen/analyze)
3. Improvised solo (listen/transcribe)
4. Head (demo)

B. Second track for each tune
1. Head (play along)
2. Solo choruses (create your own improvisation)
3. Head (play along)

You will find great solo examples to listen to and imitate. Also included are composers' insights, a discography, a list of common jazz terms and lots of licks and tricks to assist you in the process of internalizing the jazz language. Have fun memorizing these classic jazz standards.

I would like to acknowledge the support of the many individuals who have contributed time and creative energy to this series containing improvisation materials. Thanks to the efforts of Pete BarenBregge for his incredible guidance, insight and musicianship; to Bob Dingley for his inspiration, guidance and support; to Larry Clark for his vision during the early stages of development; to Bob Montgomery for his jazz arranging talent; to Shelly Berg, Ron Jolly and Javon Jackson for great written improvisations; to Paul Glessner for his research and advice; and special thanks to Willie Thomas for writing excellent improvisations and his role in helping conceive this project. To each of them I extend my sincere gratitude. Thanks to these fine musicians: Chris Vadala, Tim Leahey, Jamie Way, Ron Elliston, Dallas Smith, Paul Wingo and Clyde Conner.

NOTE: The collection of jazz riffs, rhythm patterns, harmonic concepts and much more were modeled after Willie Thomas' JAZZ ANYONE...? series (published by Warner Bros. Publications) in the preparation of materials presented in this book. Enjoy!

Dr. Willie L. Hill, Jr.

Dr. Willie L. Hill, Jr., is director of the Fine Arts Center at the University of Massachusetts-Amherst and a professor in music education. He received his B.S. degree from Grambling State University and earned M.M. and Ph.D. degrees from the University of Colorado-Boulder. He is currently president of the International Association of Jazz Educators (IAJE), president-elect of the Southwestern Division of the Music Educators National Conference (MENC), a member of the writing team for MENC's Vision 2020 and a member of the national board of directors for Young Audiences, Inc. Dr. Hill was a professor in music education and the assistant dean at the College of Music at the University of Colorado-Boulder for eleven years and director of education for the Thelonious Monk Institute. Prior to his tenure at the University of Colorado, Dr. Hill taught instrumental music and was music supervisor for 20 years in the Denver Public Schools. Professional performances in the Denver area include the Denver Broncos Jazz Ensemble, the Denver Auditorium Theater, Paramount Theater and as a freelance performer with Liza Minnelli, Lena Horne, Lou Rawls, Ben Vereen, Lola Falana, Johnny Mathis, Sammy Davis Jr., Dizzy Gillespie and many others. He is the founder and co-director of the Rich Matteson-Telluride Jazz Academy and former faculty member and woodwind specialist at the Clark Terry Great Plains Jazz Camp and the Mile High Jazz Camp in Boulder, Colorado. In 1998, he was inducted into the Colorado Music Educators Hall of Fame. He is co-author of *Learning to Sight-Read Jazz, Rock, Latin, and Classical Styles* (Ardsley House Publishers, Inc.) and the author of *The Instrumental History of Jazz* (N2K, Inc.). Hill is listed in the first edition of *Who's Who Among Black Americans* and *Who's Who Among International Musicians.*

C INSTRUMENTS
HEAD
BILLIE'S BOUNCE
LISTEN AND ANALYZE HEAD
Track 1
JAZZ DEMO
PLAY THE HEAD
Track 2
PLAY ALONG
MEDIUM BLUES
BY CHARLIE PARKER
TO CODA
1.
2.
SOLO CHORD CHANGES - 4 CHORUSES
CREATE YOUR OWN IMPROVISATION
Track 2
PLAY ALONG
F7
Bb7
F7
Bb7
F7
AFTER LAST SOLO
D.S. % AL CODA
Gmi7
C7
F7
C7
CODA

4

EXAMPLE IMPROVISATION
LISTEN AND ANALYZE

(JAZZ DEMO PLAYS 2 CHORUSES)

IMPROVISED SOLO
LISTEN, ANALYZE AND TRANSCRIBE
(JAZZ DEMO PLAYS 2 CHORUSES)

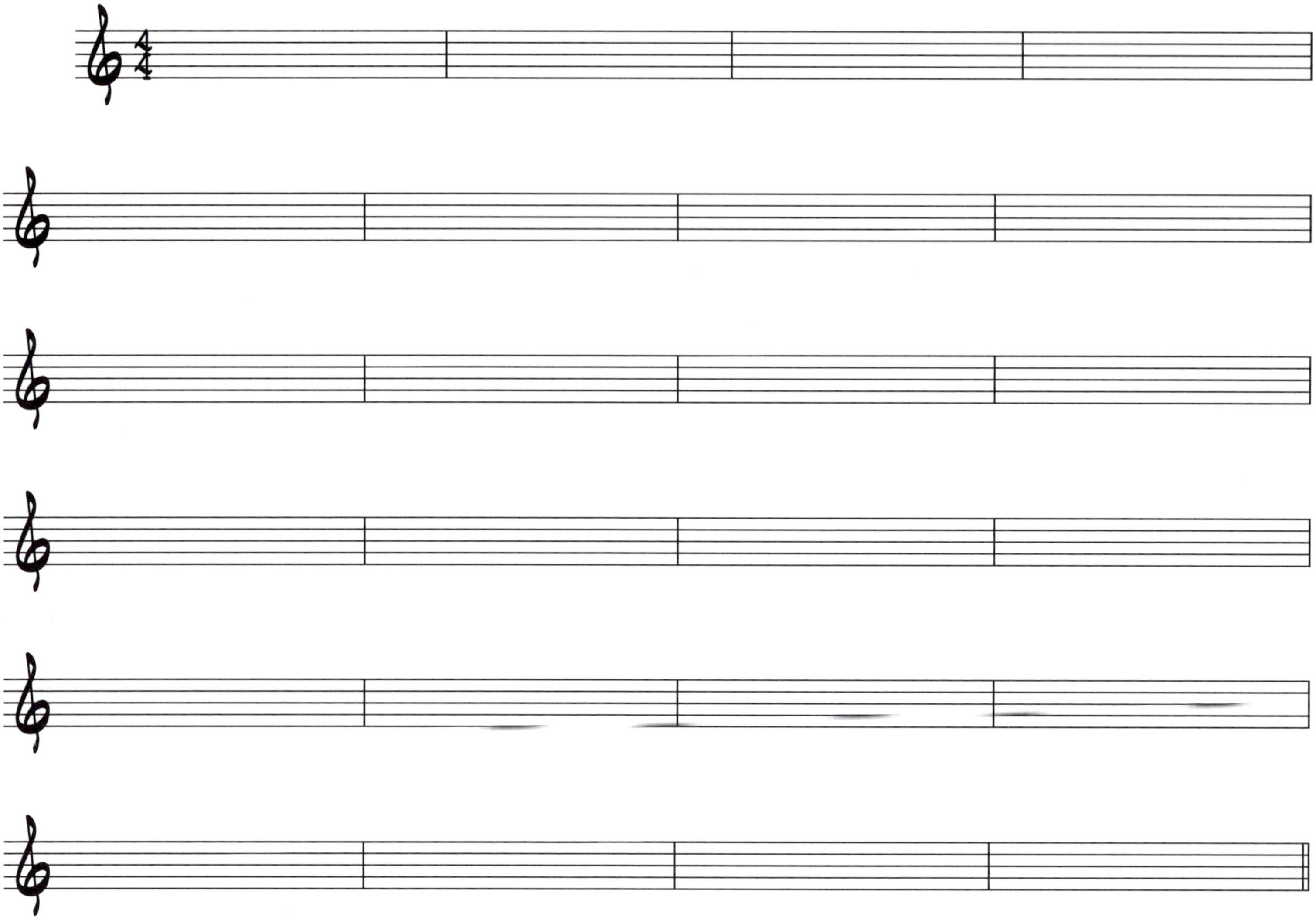

COMPOSER INSIGHT

BILLIE'S BOUNCE

Charles Christopher Parker was born in Kansas City, Kansas, August 29, 1920, and died in New York City March 12, 1955. He is one of the most influential alto saxophonists to date. Stellar compositions he penned include such jazz standards as "Now's the Time," "Scrapple From the Apple," "Ornithology," "Ko Ko," "Billie's Bounce," and a host of others. Charlie Parker was one of the founding fathers of bebop jazz. During Bird's early years, he performed in Kansas City, Missouri, in big bands, most notably with the Jay McShann Orchestra and with various R&B and jazz groups. "Billie's Bounce" is a 12-bar blues in the traditional form that uses a musical vocabulary of major, minor, and dominant 7th chords.

LICKS AND TRICKS

Lick #1 focuses on the rhythmic use of the tonic note, with figures similar to the melody line. Lick #2 is a simple riff outlining the 7th chord. Lick #3 is a bebop-style melodic line.

SCALES AND CHORDS

DISCOGRAPHY

BILLIE'S BOUNCE
Charlie Parker - *The Charlie Parker Story* - Columbia 65141
John Coltrane - *Blue Trane: John Coltrane Plays The Blues* - Prestige 11005
Red Garland/John Coltrane - *Dig It* - OJC 392
Bud Powell - *Bud Plays Bird* - Roulette 37137

On the Trail

ON THE TRAIL
C INSTRUMENTS
HEAD
LISTEN AND ANALYZE HEAD
PLAY THE HEAD
Track 3 JAZZ DEMO
Track 4 PLAY ALONG
BY FERDE GROFÉ
EASY SWING
INTRO
TO CODA
1.
2.
SOLO CHORD CHANGES - 4 CHORUSES CREATE YOUR OWN IMPROVISATION
Track 4 PLAY ALONG
F Gmi7 C7 F Gmi7 C7 F Bb Ami7 D7
Gmi7 C7 Abmi7 Db7 Abmi7 Db7
AFTER LAST SOLO
D.S. AL CODA
Gmi7 C7 F Gmi7 C7
CODA
FMAJ7(#11)

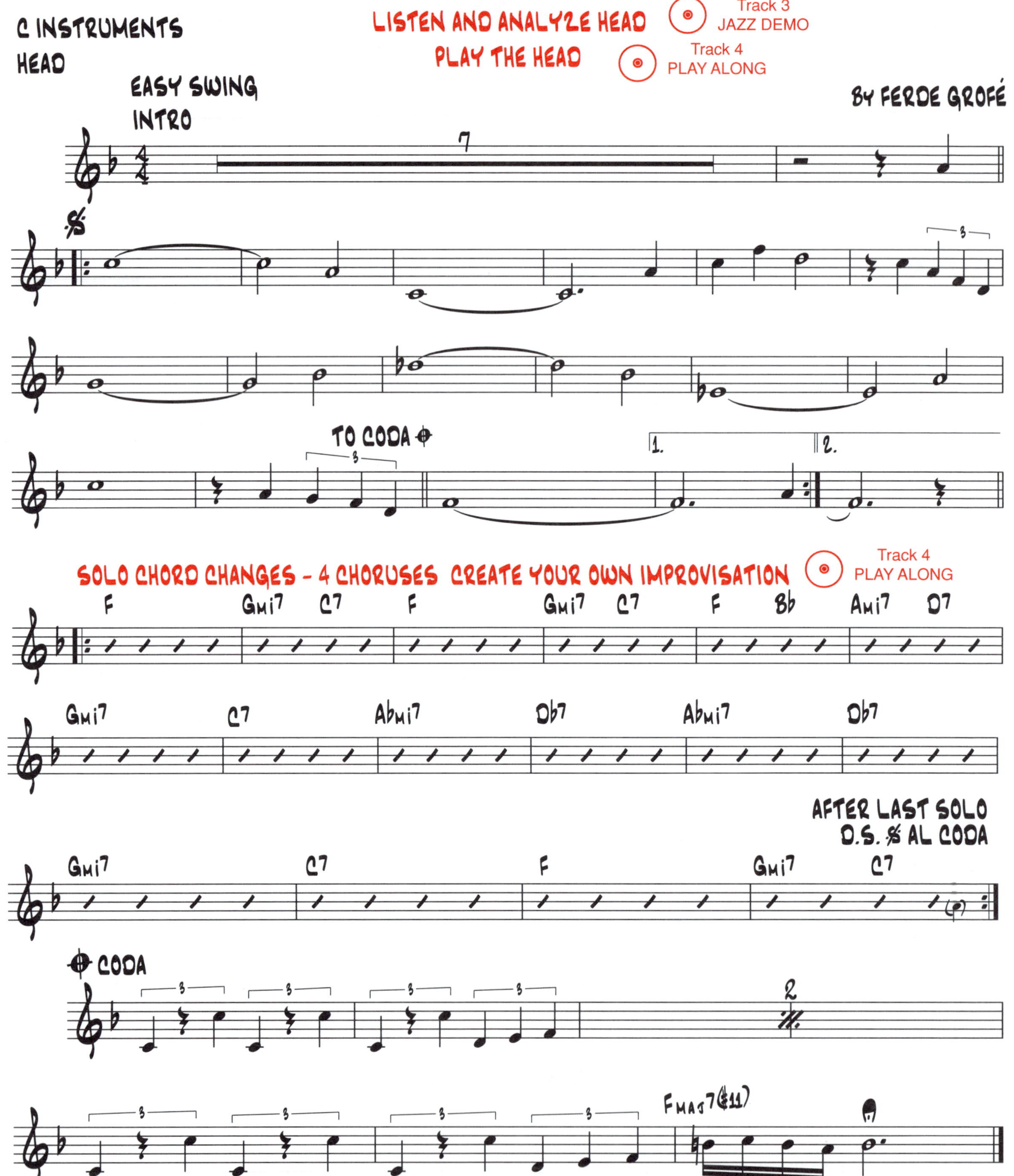

EXAMPLE IMPROVISATION
LISTEN AND ANALYZE
(JAZZ DEMO PLAYS 2 CHORUSES)

C INSTRUMENTS

BY WILLIE THOMAS

LISTEN, ANALYZE AND TRANSCRIBE — Track 3 JAZZ DEMO

(JAZZ DEMO PLAYS 2 CHORUSES)

C INSTRUMENTS

COMPOSER INSIGHT

ON THE TRAIL

The composer wrote "On the Trail" in an AB 16-bar song form. Ferde Grofé was an American composer and arranger who wrote the *Grand Canyon Suite* in 1931. He arranged compositions for George Gershwin, Paul Whiteman, and many others. His "On the Trail" has been performed and recorded by Joe Henderson, Dizzy Gillespie, Clark Terry, Harry "Sweets" Edison, The Clayton Brothers, and Tony Bennett. This tune is loaded with simple **ii-V** chord changes typical of many popular songs. A key change in the B section creates a great harmonic lift in the tune, giving players a challenge in the new key. You can play very freely through these changes with blues scales, dominant 7th scales, major pentatonics, and almost any combination of diatonic scale tones. Good rhythms and use of space make patterns work.

C INSTRUMENTS

Lick #1 is a four-measure diatonic lick. Lick #2 offers a suggested idea for the B section, a four-bar pattern that will fit over the **ii -V** chords. Lick #3 is a melodic line for the A section.

DISCOGRAPHY

ON THE TRAIL
Joe Henderson - *Four! With The Wynton Kelly Trio* - Verve 523657
Harry "Sweets" Edison - *Edison's Lights* - OJC 804
Dizzy Gillespie - *Live At The Village Vanguard* - Blue Note 80507

CANTALOUPE ISLAND

LISTEN AND ANALYZE HEAD

 Track 5
JAZZ DEMO

PLAY THE HEAD   Track 6
PLAY ALONG

C INSTRUMENTS

BY HERBIE HANCOCK

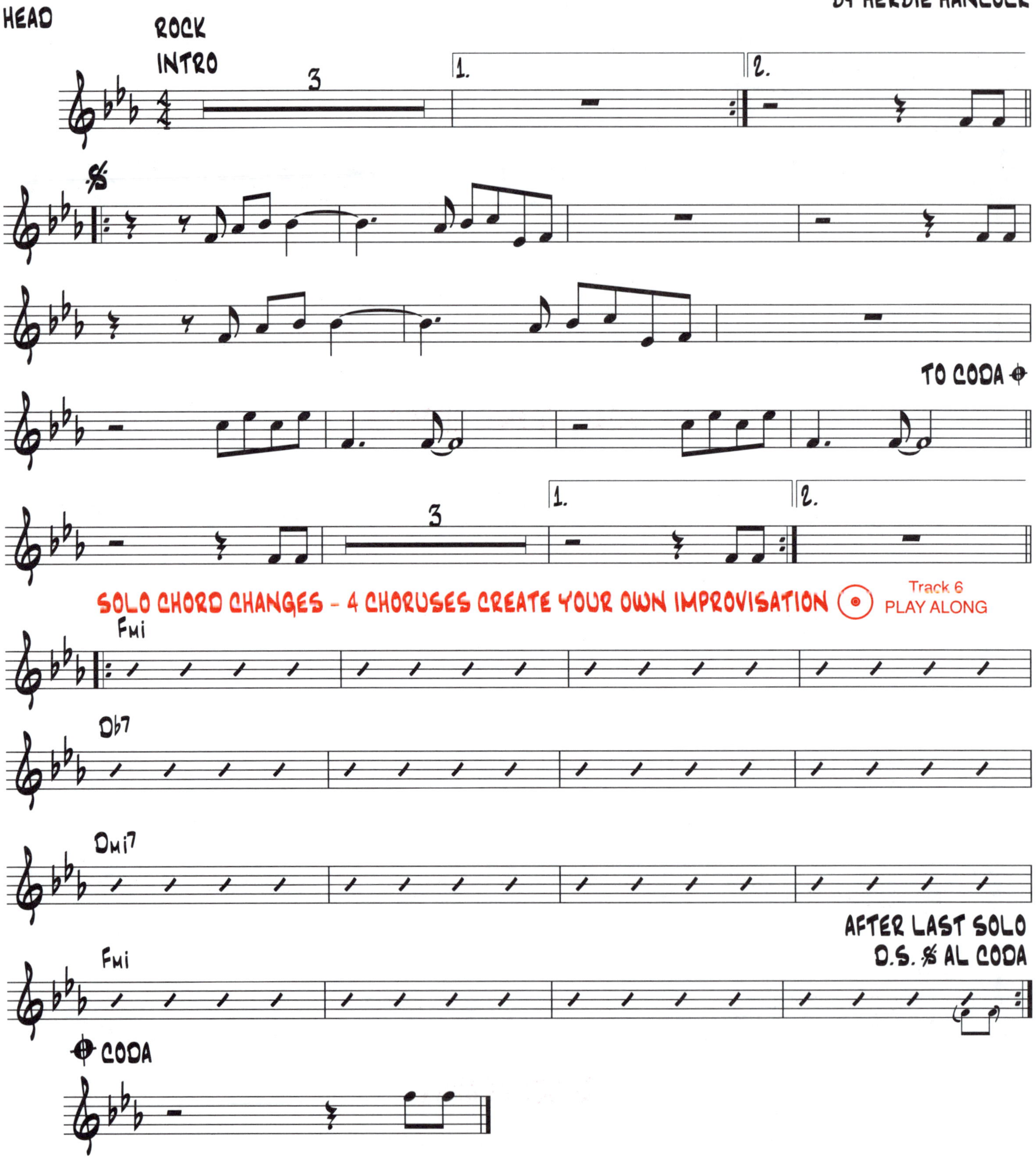

HEAD

ROCK INTRO

TO CODA

SOLO CHORD CHANGES – 4 CHORUSES CREATE YOUR OWN IMPROVISATION   Track 6 PLAY ALONG

Fmi

Db7

Dmi7

AFTER LAST SOLO
D.S. %. AL CODA

Fmi

CODA

EXAMPLE IMPROVISATION
LISTEN AND ANALYZE
(JAZZ DEMO PLAYS 2 CHORUSES)

C INSTRUMENTS

BY WILLIE THOMAS

C INSTRUMENTS

IMPROVISED SOLO

LISTEN, ANALYZE AND TRANSCRIBE

Track 5
JAZZ DEMO

(JAZZ DEMO PLAYS 2 CHORUSES)

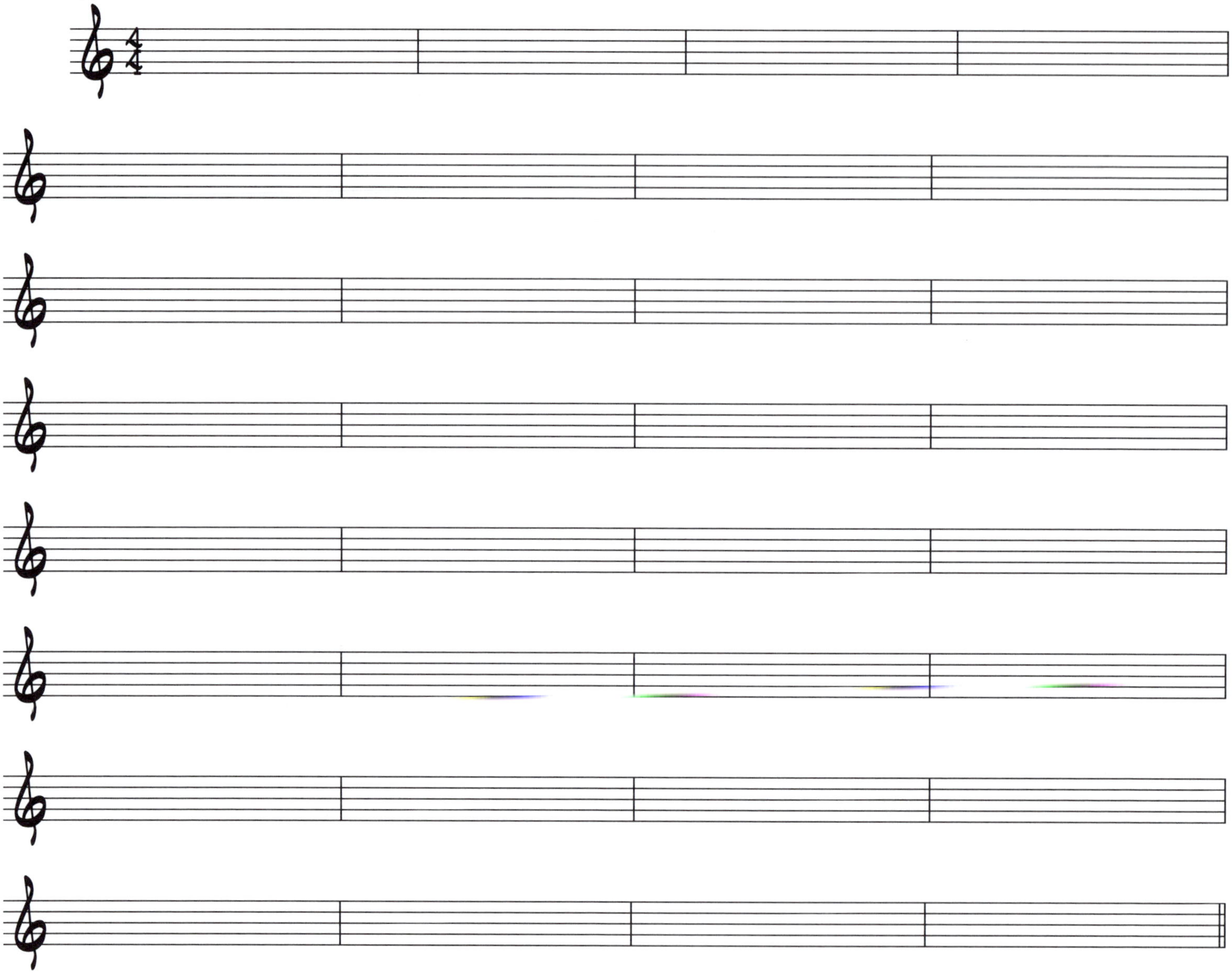

COMPOSER INSIGHT

CANTALOUPE ISLAND

Herbie Hancock is one of the greatest jazz piano/keyboard players of the twentieth century. He was born in Chicago, Illinois, April 12, 1940, and began playing the piano before he was eight years old. His jazz piano and keyboard styles include post-bop, hard-bop, modal, funk, R&B, pop, jazz-rock, and others. Hancock's well-known compositions include "Watermelon Man," "Chameleon," "Maiden Voyage," "Eye of the Hurricane," "Dolphin Dance," and "Cantaloupe Island." The latter composition is a wonderful modal tune played within a 16-bar structure, usually heard played in the jazz-rock genre. This standard uses only three different chord changes, and it has a simple yet clever melody line, allowing the player to really dig into these chord progressions. The Dorian mode produces the basic harmonic content for this piece. You can also incorporate pentatonic and blues scales to add variety to your improvisation.

LICKS AND TRICKS

Lick #1 is a two-bar phrase written as it fits in each of the three chords in this tune. Lick #2 is based on a blues scale written here for each of the three chords. Lick #3 is an eighth-note line outlining the three chords using the ninth.

SCALES AND CHORDS

DISCOGRAPHY

CANTALOUPE ISLAND
Herbie Hancock - *Cantaloupe Island* - Blue Note 29331
Herbie Hancock - *Best Of Herbie Hancock (The Blue Note Years)* - Blue Note 91143

C INSTRUMENTS
HEAD
THE PREACHER
LISTEN AND ANALYZE HEAD
Track 7
JAZZ DEMO
PLAY THE HEAD
Track 8
PLAY ALONG
BY HORACE SILVER
DOWN-HOME SWING
INTRO
TO CODA
SOLO CHORD CHANGES - 2 CHORUSES
CREATE YOUR OWN IMPROVISATION
Track 8
PLAY ALONG
AFTER LAST SOLO
D.S. AL CODA
CODA

EXAMPLE IMPROVISATION
LISTEN AND ANALYZE
(JAZZ DEMO PLAYS 1 CHORUS)

Track 7
JAZZ DEMO

BY JAVON JACKSON

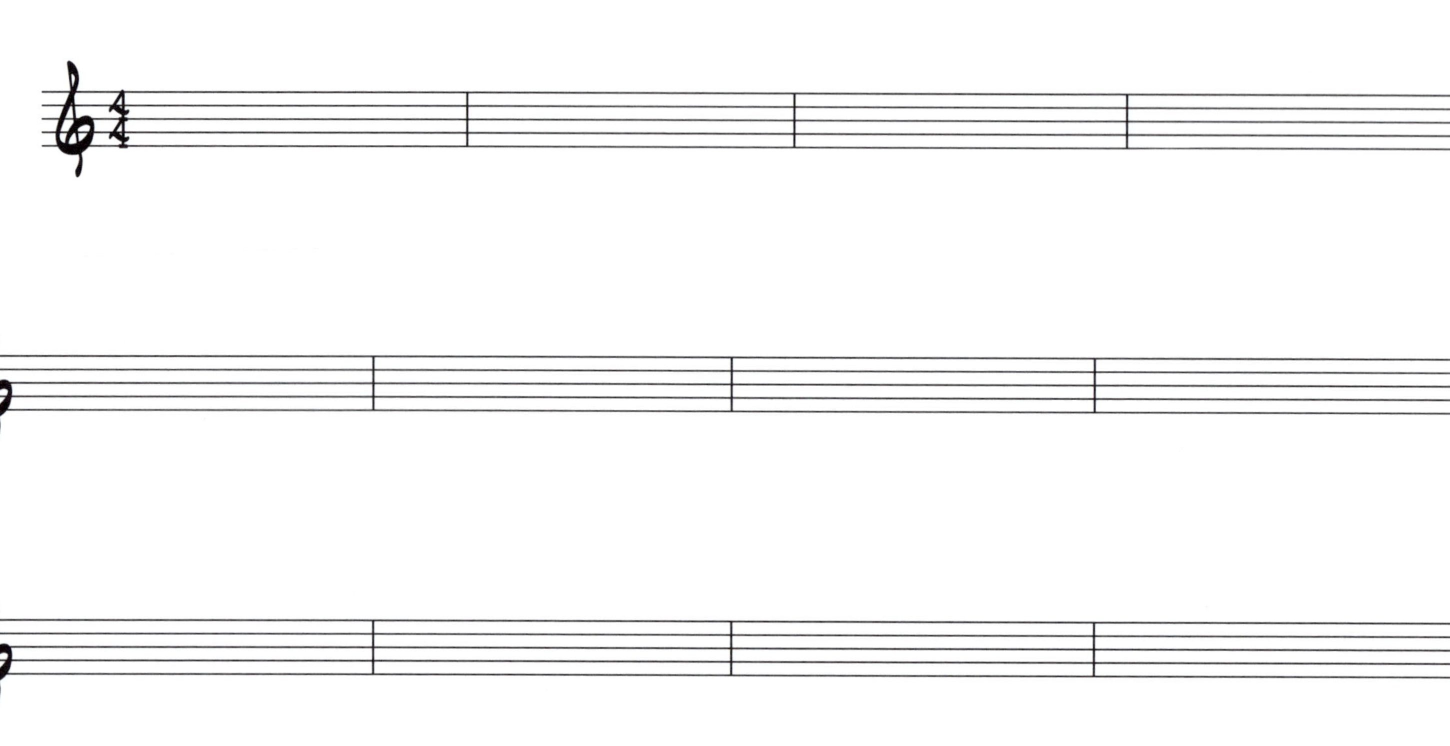

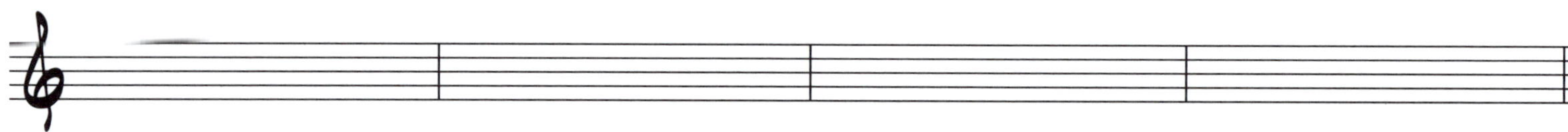

COMPOSER INSIGHT

THE PREACHER

Written in an AB 16-bar song form, "The Preacher" is one of Horace Silver's most memorable tunes. It was originally released in 1954 under the Blue Note label featuring Kenny Dorham on trumpet, Hank Mobley on tenor saxophone, co-leader Art Blakey on drums, Doug Watkins on bass, and pianist Horace Silver. Silver was born in Norwalk, Connecticut, in 1928. He is a composer, band leader, pianist, and pioneer of the hard bop era. His famous compositions include "The Preacher," "Doodlin'," "Ecaroh," "Blowing the Blues Away," "Song for My Father," "Sister Sadie," and "Peace." "The Preacher" is a happy, uplifting tune with an interesting chord progression that takes the player to the major III chord followed by a diminished chord sequence.

LICKS AND TRICKS

Lick #1 is a simple line with pick-up notes rhythmically mirroring the written melody. Lick #2 uses non-harmonic tones in a rhythmical pattern, and Lick #3 focuses on the gospel-style chord walk-up using the diminished chord in measures 13 and 14 of the tune.

SCALES AND CHORDS

DISCOGRAPHY

THE PREACHER
Horace Silver - *The Best Of Horace Silver (The Blue Note Years)* - Blue Note 91143
Horace Silver - *Greatest Hits* - CEMA Special Products 57589
Horace Silver & The Jazz Messengers - Blue Note B21 Y84175

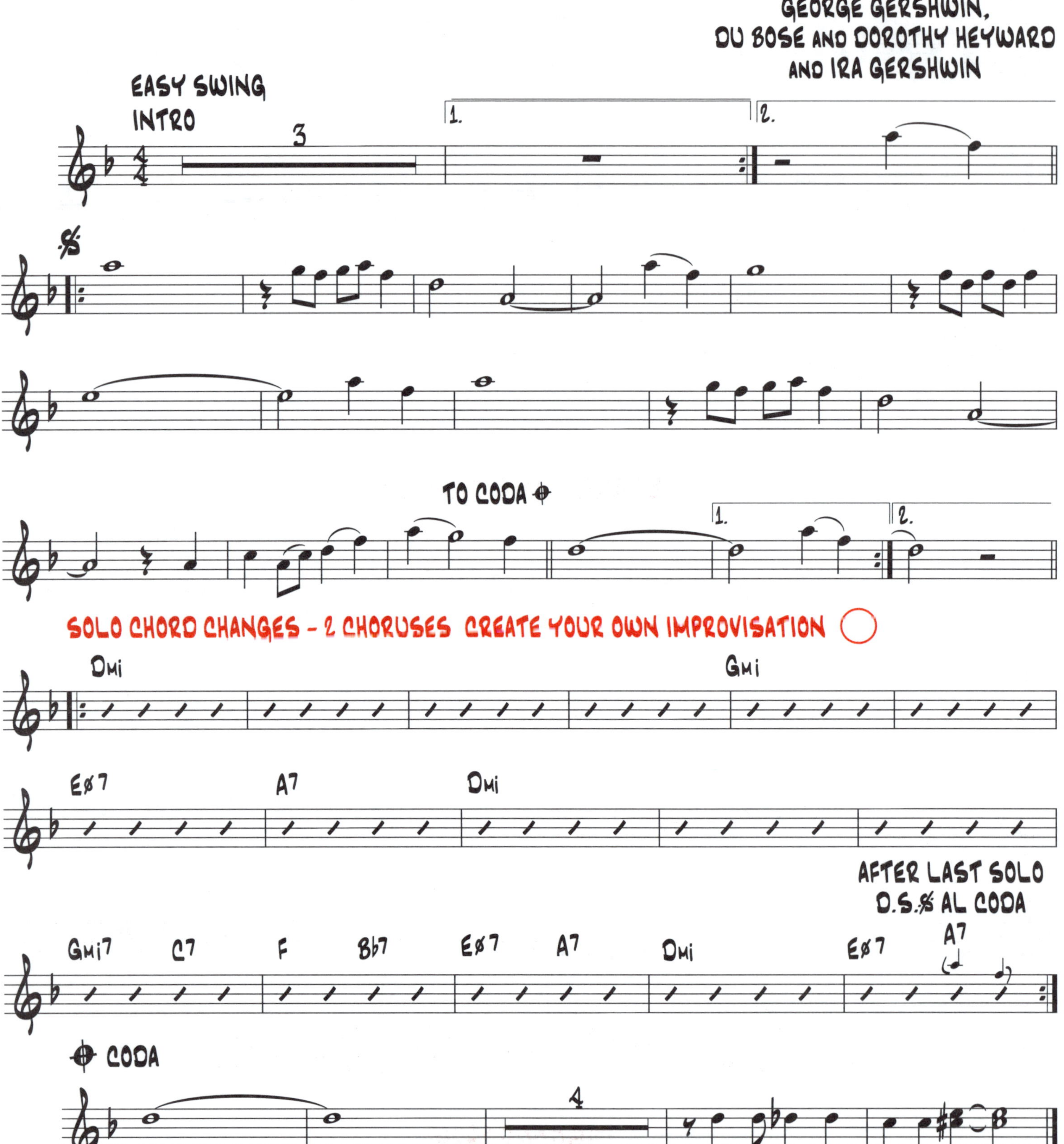
C INSTRUMENTS
HEAD
SUMMERTIME
LISTEN AND ANALYZE HEAD
PLAY THE HEAD
BY
GEORGE GERSHWIN,
DU BOSE AND DOROTHY HEYWARD
AND IRA GERSHWIN
EASY SWING
INTRO
3
1.
2.
TO CODA
1.
2.
SOLO CHORD CHANGES - 2 CHORUSES CREATE YOUR OWN IMPROVISATION
Dmi
Gmi
Eø7
A7
Dmi
AFTER LAST SOLO
D.S.% AL CODA
Gmi7
C7
F
Bb7
Eø7
A7
Dmi
Eø7
A7
CODA
4

EXAMPLE IMPROVISATION
LISTEN AND ANALYZE
(JAZZ DEMO PLAYS 1 CHORUS)
Track 9
JAZZ DEMO
C INSTRUMENTS
EASY SWING
BY JAVON JACKSON

IMPROVISED SOLO
LISTEN, ANALYZE AND TRANSCRIBE
(JAZZ DEMO PLAYS 1 CHORUS)

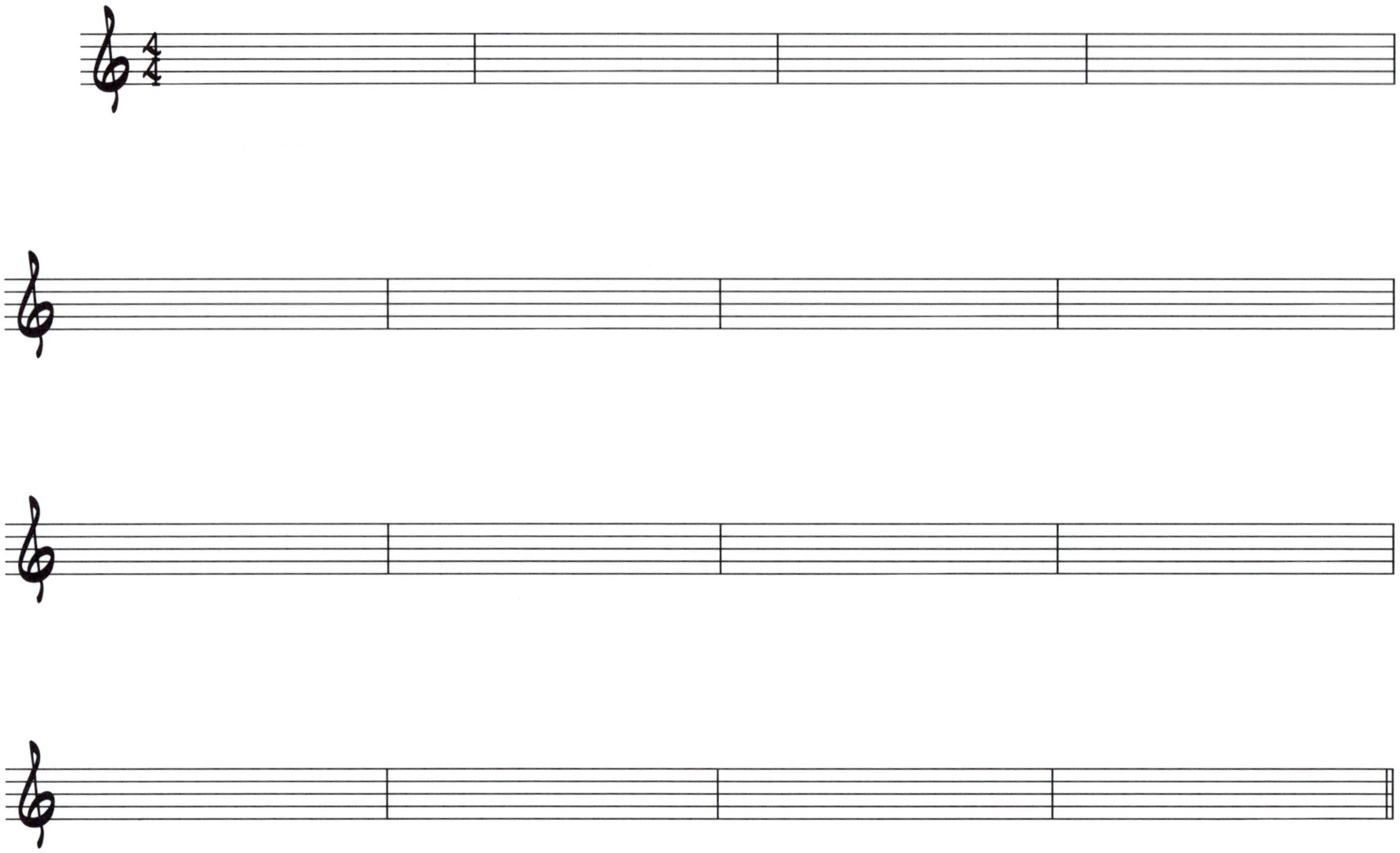

COMPOSER INSIGHT

SUMMERTIME

Porgy and Bess is a well-known American opera written in 1935 by the gifted American composer George Gershwin. From this opera, one of the most memorable tunes was "Summertime." Gershwin wrote other important works including "Rhapsody in Blue," "An American in Paris," and the tunes "Lady Be Good," "Fascinatin' Rhythm, " "Embraceable You," "I Got Plenty o' Nuttin'," "Someone to Watch Over Me," "Our Love Is Here to Stay," and countless others that jazz musicians love to "blow" over. "Summertime," a 16-bar composition usually performed in the key of D minor, is a great tune for the novice improviser because of its short and catchy melody and sparse chord changes. It offers the player an opportunity to explore non-harmonic passing tones to add harmonic variety and color. This standard has been performed and recorded countless times in a variety of settings, traditionally as a slow swing ballad.

LICKS AND TRICKS

Lick #1 is a two-bar riff that uses the descending chromatic line stated by the rhythm section; this line should be transposed to fit the other chords. Lick #2 is a simple minor melodic line, which should also be transposed to the other chords. Lick #3 focuses on the blues scale; transpose and adapt to the other chords.

DISCOGRAPHY

SUMMERTIME
Miles Davis - *Porgy And Bess* - Columbia 65141
John Coltrane - *My Favorite Things* - Rhino 45204
Chet Baker - *Compact Jazz* - Verve 840632
Bill Evans - *How My Heart Sings* - OJC 369
Charlie Parker - *The Complete Charlie Parker On Verve* - Verve 837 141-2

SATIN DOLL

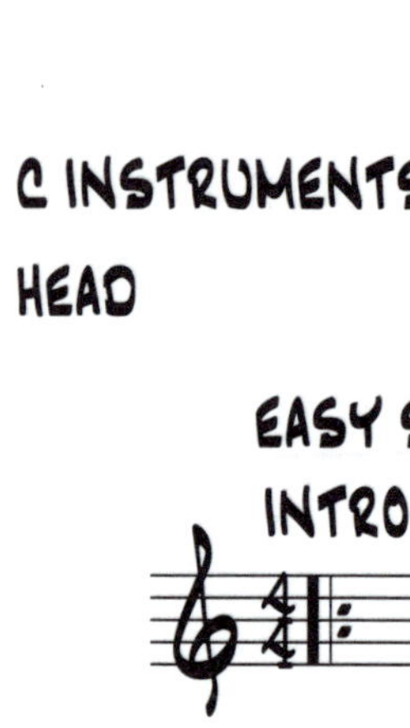

SOLO CHORD CHANGES - 2 CHORUSES CREATE YOUR OWN IMPROVISATION

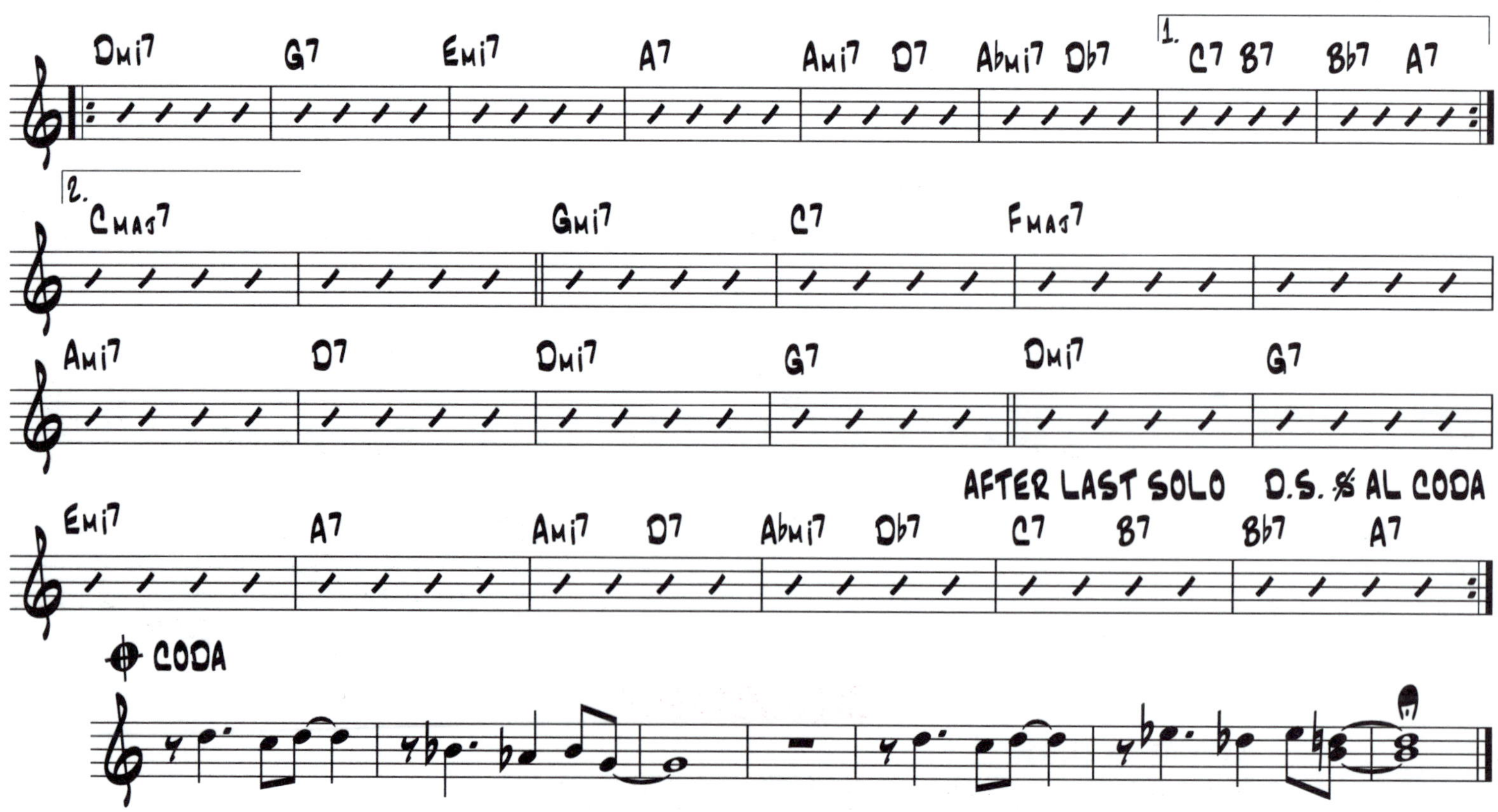

EXAMPLE IMPROVISATION
LISTEN AND ANALYZE

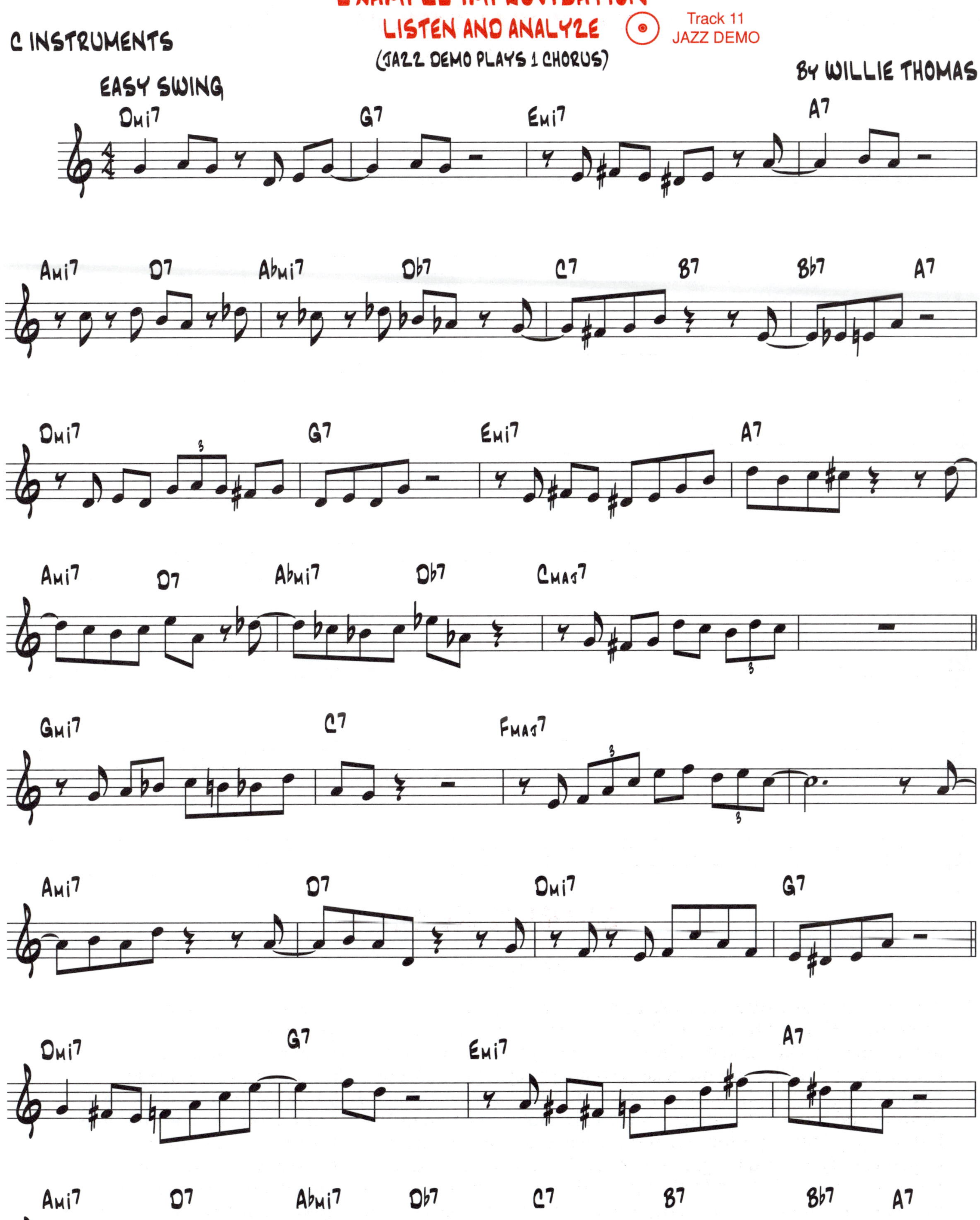

IMPROVISED SOLO
LISTEN, ANALYZE AND TRANSCRIBE  Track 11 JAZZ DEMO
(JAZZ DEMO PLAYS 1 CHORUS)

COMPOSER INSIGHT

SATIN DOLL

"Satin Doll" was written in an AABA 32-bar song form by one of this century's most prolific composers, Edward Kennedy "Duke" Ellington. Pianist Duke Ellington was born April 29, 1899, in Washington, D.C., and died in 1974 at the age of 75. He wrote thousands of tunes, many of which became a part of the jazz musician's standard repertoire. A few of his famous works include "Mood Indigo," "Sophisticated Lady," "It Don't Mean a Thing if It Ain't Got That Swing," "In a Sentimental Mood," "Solitude," and "Satin Doll." Written in 1953, "Satin Doll" was one of Duke's last hit "pop" tunes performed in the swing era style and demonstrates a variety of effective sequences. The chord progression in the A section moves the tonality up a whole-step and then progresses naturally back to the tonic. Measures 5–6 provide a traditional half-step down chord progression found in many bebop tunes. Using sequences in your improvisation will give your solos form and their own character.

LICKS AND TRICKS

Licks #1 and #2 both show a simple **ii-V** progression and are then written up a whole-step to form a sequence. Lick #3 is a quote from the Gershwin tune "Fascinatin' Rhythm" used to demonstrate a sequence. Lick #4 is a **ii-V** pattern for the bridge or B section. Transpose this pattern into the second half of the bridge. Make up your own patterns for these sequences.

SCALES AND CHORDS

DISCOGRAPHY

SATIN DOLL
Duke Ellington - *Priceless Jazz Collection* GRP 9875
Duke Ellington - *Greatest Hits* - Legacy (Columbia) 65419
Duke Ellington - *Jazz Profile* - Blue Note 54900
Oscar Peterson & Clark Terry - OJC 806
Ellington Orchestra With Mercer Ellington - *Digital Duke* GRP 9548
The Best Of Duke Ellington - Capitol 7243 8 31501

C INSTRUMENTS
HEAD

C JAM BLUES

LISTEN AND ANALYZE HEAD
Track 13
JAZZ DEMO

PLAY THE HEAD
Track 14
PLAY ALONG

MEDIUM BLUES
INTRO

BY DUKE ELLINGTON

12

TO CODA (LAST TIME)

SOLO CHORD CHANGES - 4 CHORUSES CREATE YOUR OWN IMPROVISATION
Track 14
PLAY ALONG

C7
F7
C7

F7
C7

AFTER LAST SOLO
D.S. AL CODA

Dmi7
G7
C7

CODA

EXAMPLE IMPROVISATION
LISTEN AND ANALYZE

Track 13
JAZZ DEMO

(JAZZ DEMO PLAYS 2 CHORUSES)

C INSTRUMENTS

BY SHELLY BERG

29

IMPROVISED SOLO
LISTEN, ANALYZE AND TRANSCRIBE
(JAZZ DEMO PLAYS 2 CHORUSES)

Track 13
JAZZ DEMO

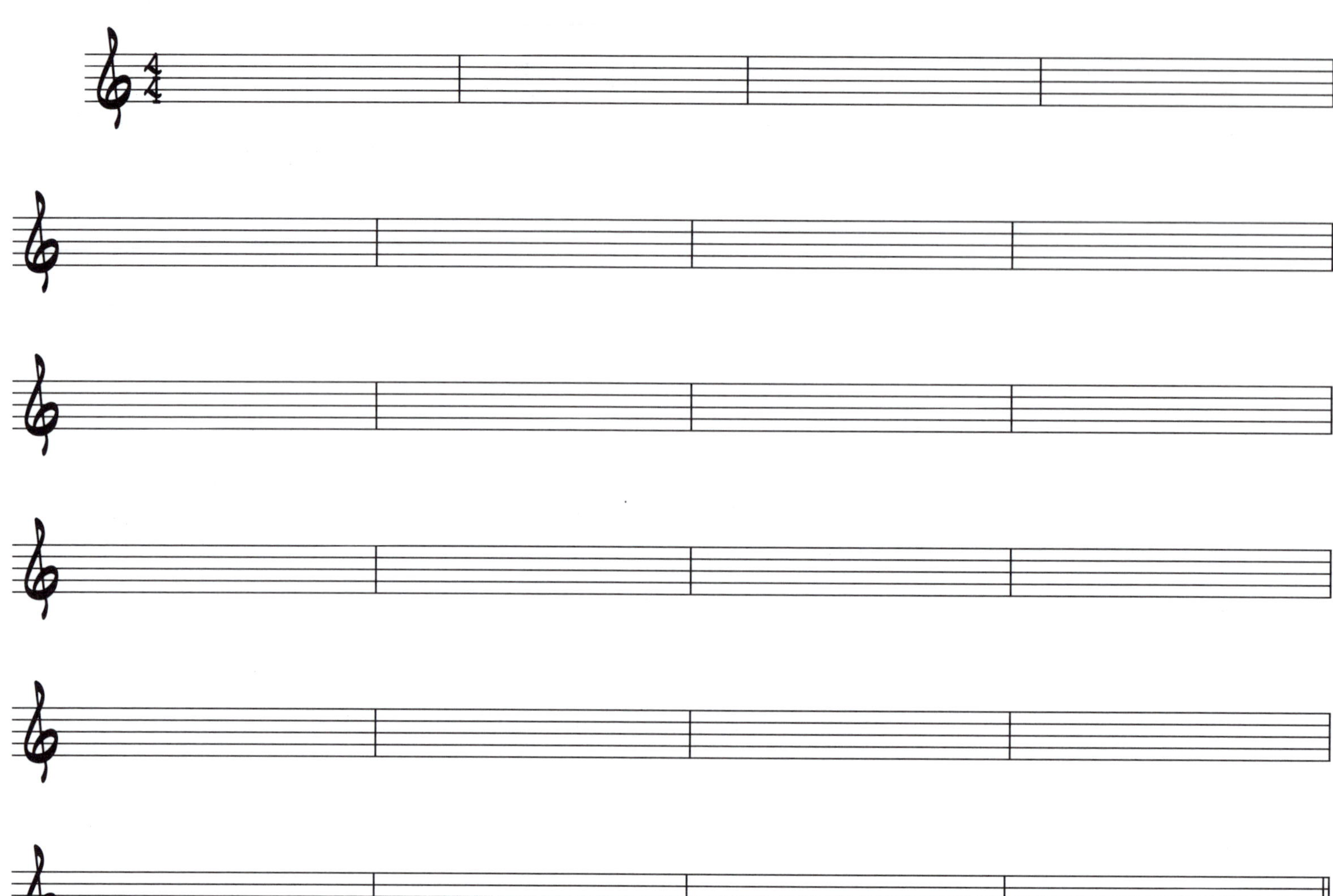

COMPOSER INSIGHT

C JAM BLUES

"C Jam Blues" is a 12-bar blues written by the master musician, composer/arranger, and pianist Duke Ellington. Edward Kennedy Ellington, better known as "Duke," born April 29, 1899, in Washington, D.C., and died May 24, 1974, in New York City, is recognized as one of the greatest jazz composers of the twentieth century. He wrote thousands of compositions, which included such jazz standards as "Sophisticated Lady," "In a Sentimental Mood," "Prelude to a Kiss," "Satin Doll," "C Jam Blues," and countless others. For more than a decade, the Duke Ellington Orchestra was the resident ensemble at the Cotton Club in New York City. A staple in every jazz player's repertoire, "C Jam Blues" is easy to memorize and can be used as a quote in other solos. Spend time working on the dominant 7th chords found in all blues progressions.

LICKS AND TRICKS

Licks #1 and #2 are both typical blues riffs that you can transpose to the other chords. Lick #3 outlines the blues scale.

SCALES AND CHORDS

DISCOGRAPHY

C JAM BLUES
Duke Ellington - *Blues In Orbit* - Columbia 44051
Duke Ellington/Count Basie - *Battle Of The Bands* - RCA Victor 63130
Benny Carter And The Jazz Giants - Fantasy 60029
The Best Of Duke Ellington - Capitol 7243 8 31501

I GOT RHYTHM

C INSTRUMENTS
HEAD

LISTEN AND ANALYZE HEAD — Track 15 JAZZ DEMO

PLAY THE HEAD — Track 16 PLAY ALONG

Music and Lyrics by
GEORGE GERSHWIN
AND IRA GERSHWIN

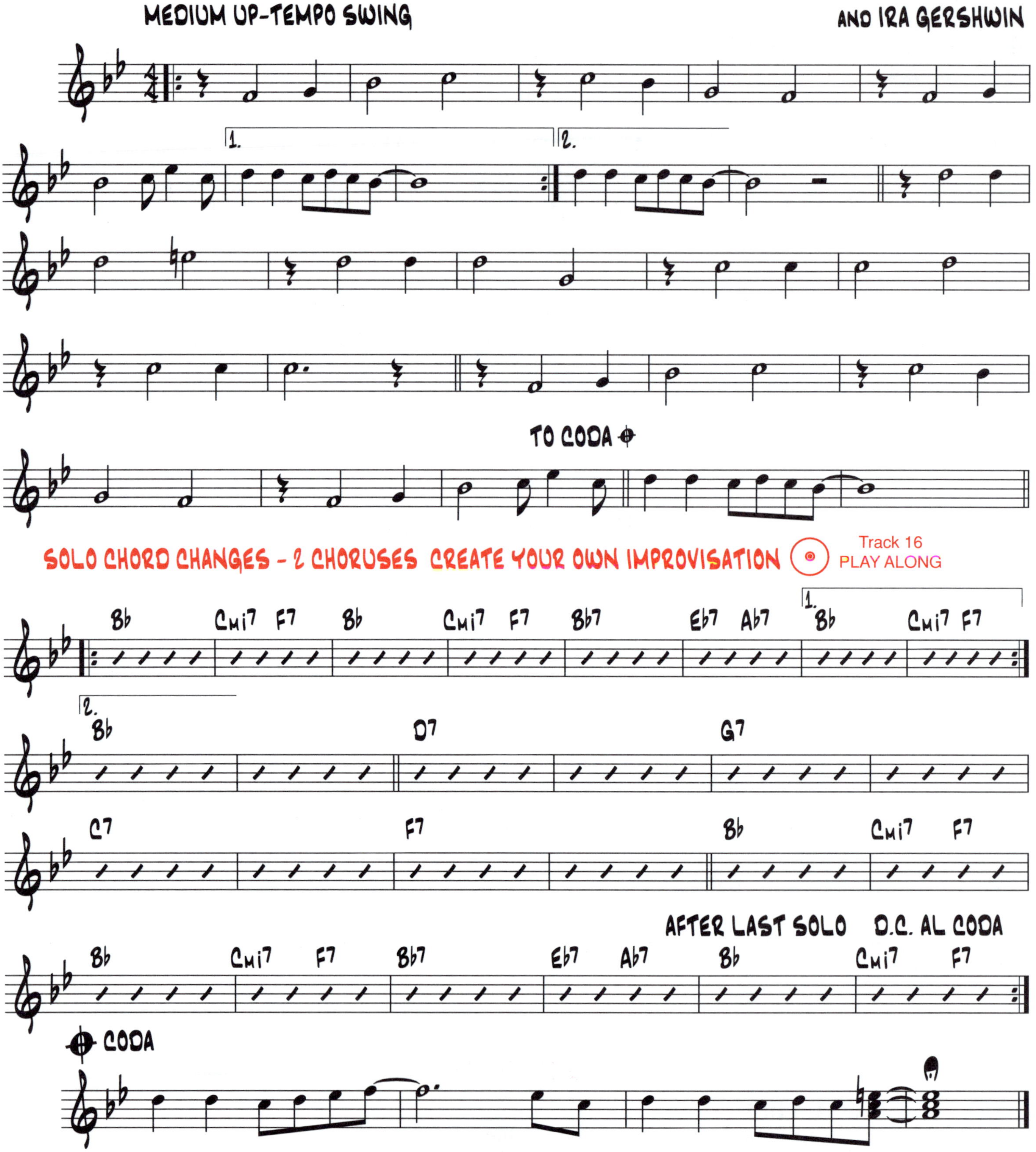

EXAMPLE IMPROVISATION
LISTEN AND ANALYZE

Track 15
JAZZ DEMO

(JAZZ DEMO PLAYS 1 CHORUS)

BY WILLIE THOMAS

IMPROVISED SOLO
LISTEN, ANALYZE AND TRANSCRIBE
(JAZZ DEMO PLAYS 1 CHORUS)

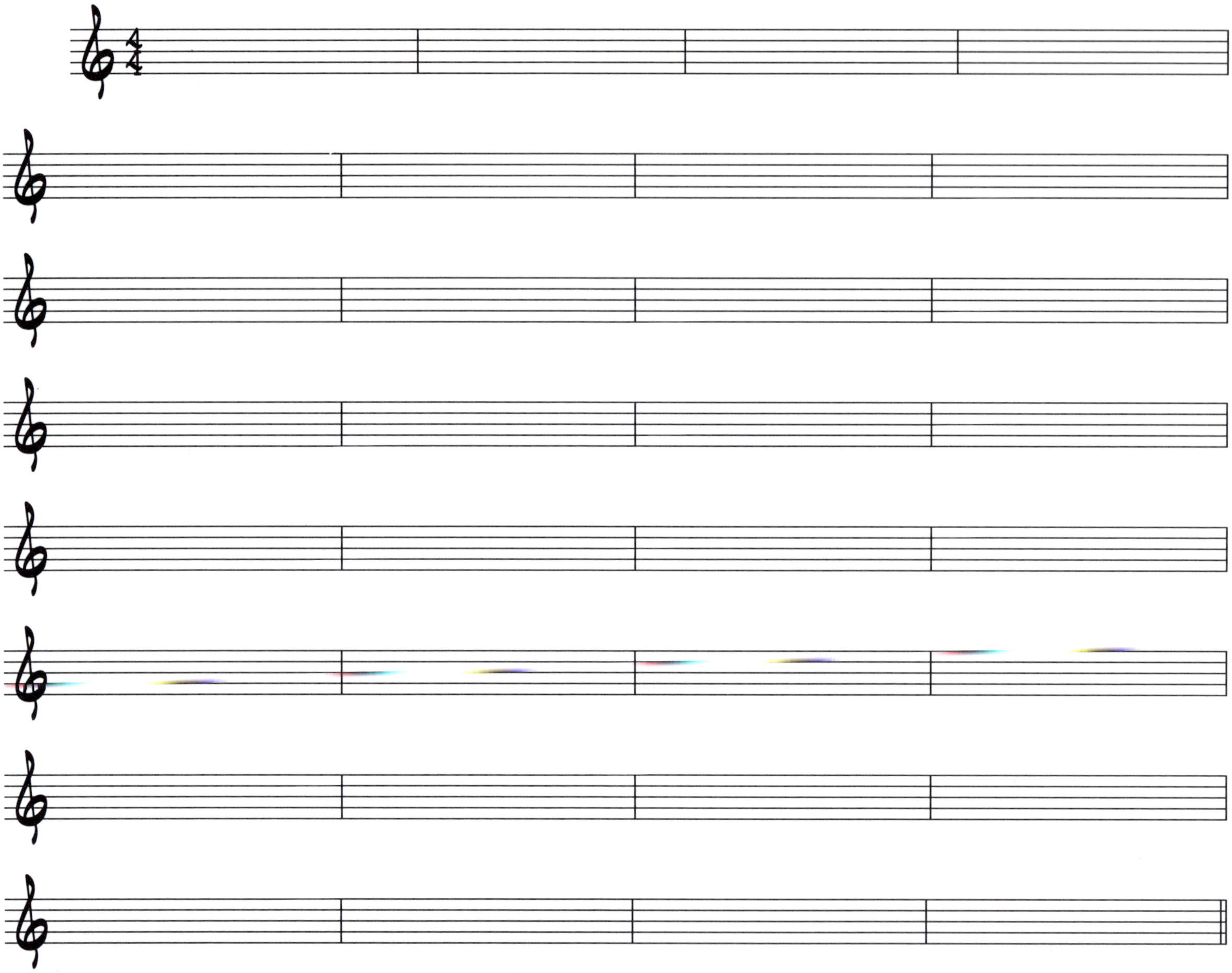

COMPOSER INSIGHT

I GOT RHYTHM

This tune was written in an AABA 32-bar song form, one of the most widely used song forms in jazz music. An extremely important set of chord changes for the jazz musician is "Rhythm Changes." These classic chord progressions are based on George Gershwin's tune "I Got Rhythm," which was written in 1930 for the Broadway musical *Girl Crazy*. Tunes such as "Oleo," "Anthropology," "The Flintstones" theme song, and many others are based on the AABA 32-bar song form. The simple diatonic chords in the A section can be played with an almost endless variety of jazz vocabulary. Dominant chords in the B section move through the circle of fourths in three keys, creating a bit of a challenge for the improviser. Since there are hundreds of tunes based on this widely used song form, you should learn this tune inside and out.

C INSTRUMENTS

LICKS AND TRICKS

Lick #1 offers a simple riff on the chord roots so the player can become familiar with the basic diatonic chord progression. Lick #2 is a pattern that flows over the **I-ii-V** chords. Lick #3 offers an idea for the bridge of the B section–transpose and continue the pattern through the other chords.

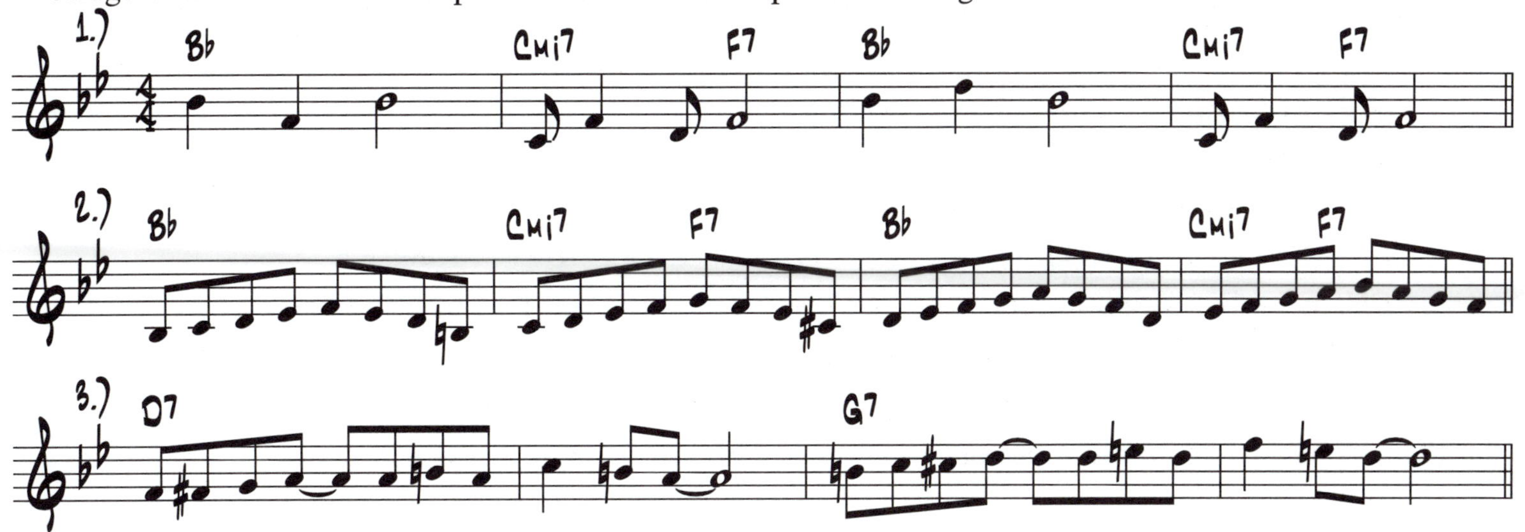

SCALES AND CHORDS

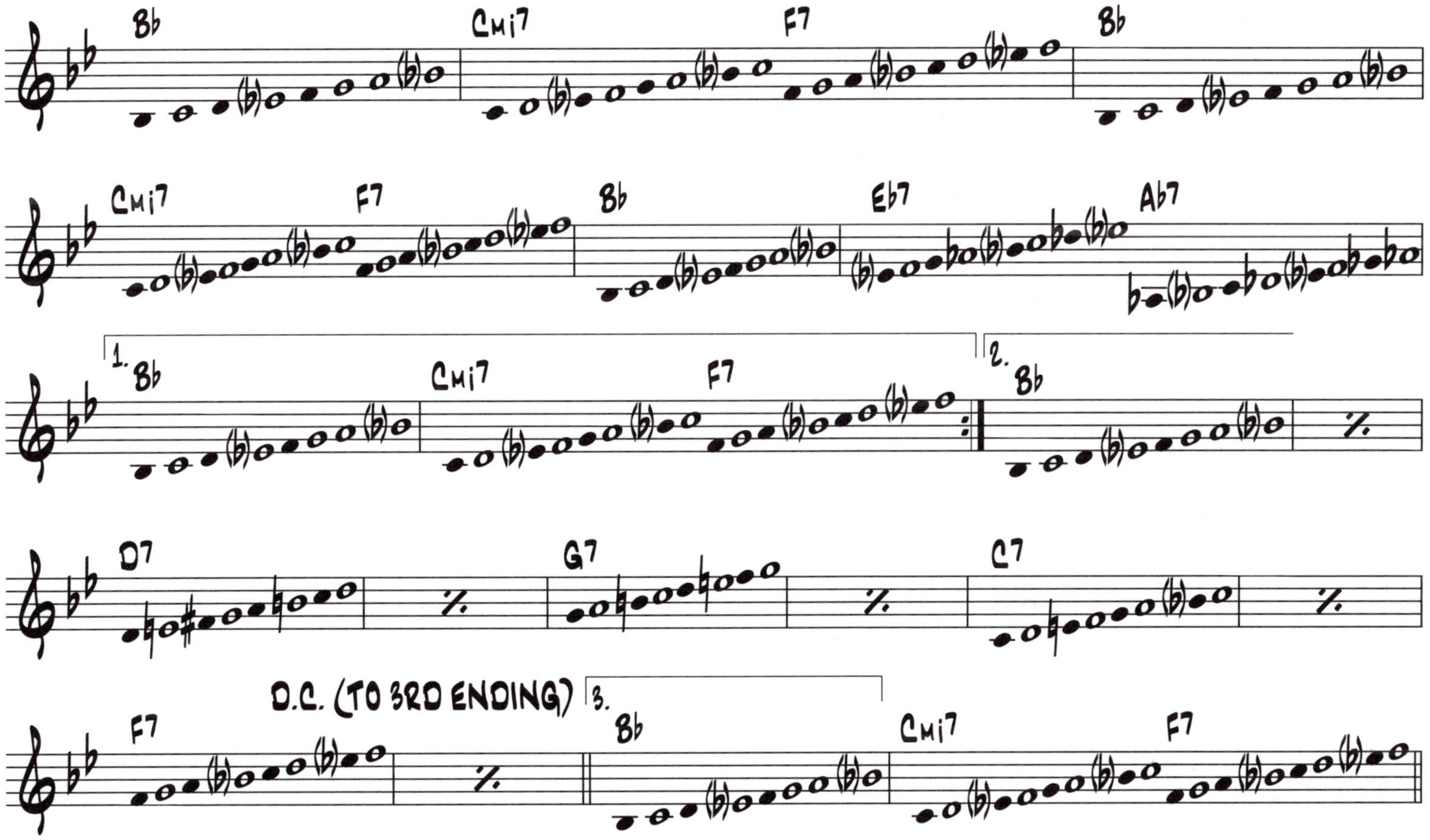

DISCOGRAPHY

I GOT RHYTHM

Louis Armstrong - *The Essential Louis Armstrong* - Verve 517169
Charlie Parker - *Ultimate Charlie Parker* - Verve 559708
Sonny Stitt - *Jazz Masters 50* - Verve 527651
Paul Chambers - *Go* - Vee Jav VJ-017

COMMON JAZZ IMPROVISING TERMS

ALTERED CHORD—A diatonic chord that has been altered by raising or lowering one or more of its elements (root, third, fifth or seventh) a half step but has not changed the function or tonality.

BLUES SCALE—1, ♭3, 4, ♯4, 5, ♭7 scale tones. No chord symbol.

BRIDGE—The B section of the AABA form, often called the release.

CHORD—Simultaneous sounding of three or more tones—1, 3, 5, 7 of scale.

CHORD PROGRESSION—Series of successive chords that accompanies the melody.

CHORUS—The form of the tune, or one time through the entire chord progression of the tune.

DIATONIC—An order of tones or intervals simply illustrated by the white keys of the piano; starting with C.

DIMINISHED SCALE—Eight-note scale with intervals consisting of WHWHWHWH.

DOMINANT 7th CHORD—A major-minor seventh chord built on the fifth scale degree in either major or harmonic minor tonality, 1, 3, 5, ♭7.

LICK—A short musical idea or motive.

HALF DIMINISHED SCALE—Seven-note scale with intervals consisting of HWWHWWW.

HEAD—Melody.

IMPROVISATION—Creating musical ideas played over the chord progression. Scales, chords, rhythms and tune melodies are guides.

NON-HARMONIC TONES—outside the diatonic scale or key.

PATTERN—Also referred to as a segment, a short musical phrase repeated.

PENTATONIC SCALE—Five-note scale.

RIFF—Short musical idea repeated.

SEQUENCE—A systematic transposition of a motive to different scale degrees. It may be literal (modulating) or diatonic (non-modulating).

TONIC NOTE—Keynote of scale or first degree of scale.

WHOLE TONE SCALE—Six-tone scale, each interval a whole step.

I, IV, V CHORDS, ETC.—Another more traditional way to notate chord progressions. This notation provides a broader perspective on chord relationships. Numeral refers to scale tone. Major=upper case, minor=lower case.